...amily

With high regards
and deep affection

Larry Clark

SPEAK TO THE EARTH

by
Larry Roger Clark

DORRANCE & COMPANY
Philadelphia

For My Wife
Ida Ruth

Speak to the earth,
and it shall teach thee.

Job 12:8

CONTENTS

Page

I. MOODS AND LOVE

FRIENDS

Friendship is the sharing of a dream,
Or maybe just a moment's thoughtfulness
Between two, passing through the aisle of time.
A smile transmitted in a pressing hour,
Or teardrops in the rain.
So short a time is granted us
To delve into a person's far-off thoughts—
To really sense we know our friends—
That we must catch the glimpses as they come,
Before they pass beyond our way.
Friendship is a captured hope
Fresh from a poet's soul,
A simple understanding in the silent hour,
A pleasure in the sunlight,
A hand clasped in the crowd.
These are the friendships that are ours.

ON MONDAY

I like you, Ida;
And radishes,
And mornings 30° below.
I lay thinking of you, shortly before dinner;
We had soup today, and brown bread,
And radishes of course.
I thought of what it would be like to leave you;
Tears came!
And I realized how much more I love and need you
Than ever before.
I need the special way you have of showing,
Without saying it, that you love me,
When we love.
I need the hope you give
Of that better day ahead.
I thought about Iowa, Hawaii, Lake Superior
And crackers for my soup;
Of new houses and old friends, now gone;
Of butterflies with silver wings.
I thought about many things,
But mostly about you!

LOVE IS

Love is feeling
The clouds of the soul
Driven with mighty wind;
Seeing spring before it comes,
Realizing green life beneath snowbanks,
Light beyond darkness,
Dreams amid pain.
Love is finding you,
And having you stay close.
It is laying down my private schemes
In favor of you;
Stroking sunlight through your hair.
Love is beauty that surrounds
The forever dawn.

AND THEY LOVED

They loved the denser forest
Running out beyond the traveled path,
Their walks that led them back
To sense and singleness;
Their cherished words of love
Fleeced by the breath of snow,
Forever guarded by the height of Norway pine.
They loved the chickadee
That flitted from jack to birch
And up beneath spruce boughs
Bearing heavily under white.
They loved the night,
And each other;
The murky haze of slush covering the moon.
They loved pinecones and icicles,
The snow packed on the north side of the house—
And they loved.

WITH YOU

I'm with you when amber light
Slants through late afternoon windows,
And a thread of tears of remembrance is held back
By only the slightest silken fiber.
I'm with you for the mile of life's untrodden track,
And when the heart is leaping back
To childhood's innocence and charm.
When thoughts are piled high
With dreams and new adventures,
Then I am there—to share these inner beauties.
I'm with you through somber hours,
When souls refined and polished
Reflect that great eternal light.
I'm with you in the night
When life is stilled with moonlight
Cutting patterns on bird nests,
And cool grass breaths.
I'm with you in the morning of each fragile day
When pink dispels the gray,
And flowers unfold their joyous heads.
I'm with you at these times,
For I am with you—always.

LOVING

Forgive me for loving without showing,
For feeling without knowing,
For suppressing what is growing.
I'm cast down to have hurt thee when
I could not tell thee why.
Repent I that I ever laughed, or
Looked up to the sky,
If I would hide within, what made
Me breathe and love and cry.
I know that words, though meant, cannot repair
Unless they grasp the yearning one did bear,
And give it back to one who was so near.

LOVE

Deep love is that quality of the will
That does not come suddenly,
But steadily in the line of growth.
It is neither the inrushing of an overpowering
Emotion or a superficial flower to beautify a life,
But rather the overflow of a soul made glad—
The fruit of a truly satisfied life!
In this sense, love is a complete and stable
Element of life.
We depend upon our family for many years
After we are born. Throughout this time
Of dependence we are learning to love them.
And the love grows increasingly and is enhanced
Through the years of kinship and maturity.
In years to come this is the essence of love
We really desire in friendships formed.
Not the burst of immaculate passion,
But the development of that unquenchable
And unchanging will of the heart!

CHANGING PHILOSOPHY ON A METHOD OF LIVING

Goals to me, before,
Were like flashing neon signals to pursue.
Not any more!
Goals are no longer something I desperately follow after;
For the goals are within me, being worked out,
Constantly in the process of change.
Now, it is not living life in the pursuit of happiness,
But rather, being happy here and now;
Living the life with ease
Rather than compounded frustration.
Not following after life,
But letting life follow after me;
Nor taking the art of living in my hands
Compressing it to fit my needs,
But letting the essence of daily living mold my life
In the process of its living fulfillment.

LONELY

Loneliness is a bird high in flight
Circling a deserted canyon;
Or the mind high in thoughts
Of the remembered closeness
Of a far friend.

The turmoil of the mind
Finding no answers,
And living with this fact.

Loneliness is the misty dusk
Sliced through by razor-edged swampgrass;
The sudden realization
Of the pattern of one's existence,
And its futility.

It is all one's ambitious dreams
Caught in an unexpected downpour,
Or a person's will refusing to face
The confrontations of a more meaningful reality.

Loneliness is approaching God as a stranger.

PESSIMISM

The vanity of years
The countenance of time
The ceaseless motion of the spheres
And all is left behind.

The cruelties of dawn
The hopelessness of change
The never ending song
Of an eternal age.

The fitful birds of space
The frightened man of days
The years have methods to erase,
Tomorrows have their ways.

The canticles of life
Are written in the sand;
The meaning of another age
Thrust in a child's hand.

DESPAIR

The moon was sliced as was the brutal world
that stifled hour. The air was silent, but
evil fed upon the quiet noon of night. The
sky was waiting for that silver semisphere
to disappear. Then the flood of captured life
would break upon the world. The heartless
spaces uttered twelve words of an unhealthy
church chime. The joy of life was fleeing
on tempestuous wings. It is noble to die
a quick-ending death of utter loss steeped in
injustice.

II. MINNESOTA

RENEWED HOPE

When I opened my eyes to rafters of tree limbs,
I forgot who I had been before,
And became what I was then—
A friend to the pine,
And a friend to God.
I enjoyed the sobriety of cold morning air
Towards too early a visitor of spring,
And saw parcels of white
Pocketed in bowls of decadent leaves.
The fire was my companion of the night,
Until the welcome of the early sun.
Now I am enjoying two warmths.
Trees of white are flourishing birchbark banners.
Nearby, jackpine logs linger in repose.
I sense:
    The ridge upon which I sit, pineneedles,
    The dark-wet earth with roots immobilized,
    The lake, surging with white-capped dreams,
    The campfire, enclosed by a circle of bricks,
    And renewed hope.

A CHERISHED PAIN

I'm walking in the woods with you, awhile,
Down fragrant scented lanes,
Where beauty softly breaks to bud
From winter's strict domain.

I'm walking after summer rain,
When every leaf is dripping dry.
I'm dreaming in the freshened air,
And never asking why.

I'll stop to sit upon a stump
With blueberries grown round,
And listen to an ancient owl,
And gaze upon the fertile ground.

So I have walked with you this day,
Though miles are far between,
And shared the wonders of the woods
Where friends are often seen.

BACKYARD BIRCH

The birch behind the house
Had let the snow run up its trunk this year.
Oh, it was posing in its normal arching stance,
But other years had not allowed
Such familiarity to chance.
Was this a yardful of special snow,
More powdery, imposing special favors?
I did not think my white-clothed friend was growing old
To where he would let down his guard
Against the frozen cold; Although this may have been
His case as moss had through the years bearded
His weathered face,
And only on his upmost trunk was seen the
Hope of white-curled bark.
His lower dress was dark
With landmarked age.
The snow clutching him
May have been a camouflage
Against the wind,
But I presume the gust was friend
As it swung his ice-twigged branches now and then,
Above a line of snow-shoe tracks.
I like to think my cheeks were rosy with delight
Of having paid a visit to a friend
And not the cold that made them bright.

EMBERS AND LOGS

Half-burnt logs vanishing from the bottom up
Look as if they are arching from the heat,
Being heavily chalked with cracked ashes.
Clinging to the logs, tails of ashes
Are tiny banners of clouds in an ethereal sky.

Orange ash chips beneath have covered themselves
With blue blankets that are vibrating gently.
A mantle of caked darkness
Adorns the backs of the patient martyrs
Who are making silent cracklings.

A slight issue of smoke responds
To the questing blackness above.
On the floor of the fire
Lies the living rubble of a hundred dreams.

THE VEILED WOODS

Coming to the veiled wilderness
Whose edge, the untaught eye can only see,
The foliaged tree,
The thicketed entanglement of growth,
The insects buzz to loathe,
The windfalls of the humbled trail;
These, but the draperies of the veil
Which hide the greater share of worth,
The more eternal
Veiled by the vestiges of earth.
The far wilderness is but the mask
Of the pure wings of thought,
The great wellspring of an unformed inspiration,
The wisdom to be taught of quietness and beauty.
Discretion and contentment concealed under
Quiet-pearled dew.
Love and comfort clinging in the
Tender jewelweed springing, green and new.
Finding peace of mind
Beside a giant, towering pine;
Or feeling single grace
In thread of spider web
Across the face.
Restoring of the soul upon a clover scented knoll.
Walk with wisdom there,
And you will find an end of all despair.

MINNESOTA MORNING

I walked out this morning
Under crystalled skies
To where a world breathed cold.
Life was stilled to essential immobility;
The sun frozen in mid-sky.
As I shoveled brittle chunks of snow
Against a snow-plowed bank,
They became cinders
Clattering down a railroad embankment.
Wind, mustering up my breath,
Whipped it bitterly around my face.
A nearby jackpine snapped at me
Like the retort of a rifle.
Trees stood head-high in distilled blue vastness,
Motionless in outer space.
Soon, sharp cracklings of treetop branches
Reechoed through stands of rigid timber,
As the ghost of new snow moved stealthily down
From high, laden boughs.
Two ancient iceboxes lay vacant,
Domed with tiered reminder
Of every past snowfall.
I will walk out again
When it is colder.

STAR-BOUND

Outside tonight,
I breathed of magnificent wind
And gazed on an ocean of stars
With men and maidens through the centuries.
I marveled of the same eternal distant light,
Feeling cool wind as they did on
Sheep covered slopes ages ago.
Making me conscious of my smallness
Beneath this vast ocean,
A single blazing burst of white
From one streaking star
Extinguished itself into quick darkness.
I felt, trembling on my lips,
A momentary and eternal wish
Of love towards the one I loved.
I let waves of wind wash over
This fragile pebble on the shore.
Hark! The trees are listening.
I will not spoil the woods with words.

SNOW

Sunlight filtering through
Snow-clouds banked against the western sky.
The dew of snow seen fluttering
In diffusion as it leaves its
Abode of pines;
Or in the blustery gusts of a new-blown storm,
Seen dropping greatly from high reaching boughs.
And as the storm and night come on,
Darkened white swirling at the corners of
The cottages of light and bedding down
In heavily packed repose.
Frost climbing window panes
As cold bites down.
In a world without, the stealthy trees
Slide out to hide amid the circling storm.
All through the wild, surging night
New heights of snow are born
Until the cautious morning comes, creeping in,
To see what mischief night has done.
With it comes a calm one does not dare to touch
For at least an hour—just simply to behold.

A LONELY LAKE–SUPERIOR

The moon was high and hostile in the hushed night sky.
Fear-fraught clouds had fled before their enemy, the moon.
Only one line of night-clouds, paralyzed with loneliness,
Lay huddled on the far Wisconsin shore.
A cascade of semi-darkness
Wrestled with the rocky water's edge.
The persistent trees tightened their grip upon the shore,
Imbedding their roots upon the rock-ledged land.
Moss-greened molars of rockblack reefs
Poised in waiting below the waterline;
Granite teeth to wolf down the intruding land.
This night would reveal its slippery,
Purple-washed landmarks of solitude;
The bursting spray sending its flying teardrops up
Over the veritable sentries,
To diffuse on the apprehensive voice of the midnight wind;
Its strip of shell-rolled beach
With the overhanging inquisitiveness of the maple
And the dignified self-resignation of the pine.
This was a lonely lake–Superior.

IMPRESSIONS OF THE CAMPFIRE

The fire posts a vigil
Against the tongues of creeping darkness.
Wind brushes up from off the surface of the lake;
Pines above lisp welcome.
A lone mosquito pleads awhile, then disappears.
The firefly signals his domain.
Earlier, a deer leaped across the road and by the spring.
The ground beneath the sleepingbags is needle strewn.
Bear live in this wood.
The rain sheds a few drops of love.
Birds see which one may say the last goodnight,
Everyone else is asleep.
With flame now gone,
Smoke twists up into tree limbs.

JANUARY DUSK

Gray sky was frozen over in the west
As day lay upon its deathbed.
There was not a breeze of hope
That the frozen agony would end.
The world had ceased moving
And was dying slowly where it stood.
One could not see the sun, nor sense
Even the meekest signal of its hospitality.
Everything was gray.
As I thought, this grayness grew upon me,
For I was part of the world,
The world was part of it,
And it was insistent in its demand
That all conform to it.

NELSON LAKE

Traveling in by motor bike made the leaves chatter on the two-laned trail behind. The hills this fall seemed even more rocky and steep than they were in summer. Maybe it was because the road was letting its washouts go untended. At any rate I had to shift into first to make the last hill. At the lake, the deer-track around the south side asked me if I'd like to walk it. So I did. I wasn't disappointed even though my feet often turned on the rocks in the path. A fallen birch across the trail forced me to sit on it and swing my legs over. The water was quiet today, and yellow leaves lost from the others floated on the surface of the lake near shore. When I got to the point of land with the great granddad white pine on it, I knew it was time to turn back. All along the shore the birches were leaning this way and that. Some peered into the water wondering what might be beneath. The poplar leaves still in trees on the hills above were gold and rust. When I got back to my bike, I paused. Nearby was a camping site. The sun warmed me as I sat down on the picnic-table for a moment to think.

FLEECE OF SNOW

Stillness settled
As frosty feathers parachuted earthward,
The fleecy brilliance of crystalled darkness
Borne by the northwind,
The lightest whisper of an eternal dream,
Fallen to the earth,
To this very frozen ground
On which my feet will lightly tread.
These will be the hopes of men:
This eternal breath of the northland,
The frosted silences,
And the wonder to behold.

SUN AND SILENCE

Wood huddled under habitation
Of the January cold;
Sawed-up into stovepipe lengths,
Memorial to a balsam
Uprooted by a summer's storm,
Now, content to shiver
Piled and capped by winter's form,
With only light ringed ends exposed;
Skirted by tracks of animals
Which dared to brave the drifts.
The only other guise was this,
The sun, the silence—and the sapling spruce.

WINTER ALDER BRUSH

The alder brush are weeping on the ground
With iced eyes. The snows laid torturous
Burdens on their bending backs.
The brush are crying on the rabbit tracks.
Their branching heads frozen down,
Buried or half-hidden in white crusted ground.
Now and then they murmur,
Upon remembering summer,
And dote upon the day when they shall rise,
And lift again their heads into warm skies.

DUSK IN SPRING

The dusk will have its way,
It is useless to resist.
Delicate splotches of pink sky
Creep cautiously behind the web of darkening gray.
Open water on the lake between the ice floes
Reflects only the pink of the sky
As if some protest against the gray.
Yardlights are coming on at houses in the wood,
To contradict the dusk's persistent voice.
Trees are swaying too, like some young child
Who thinks it is not time to go to bed.
Wind, agreeing with the dusk,
Is making its cold fingers known.
The woods and air have clothed themselves in gray,
It is useless to resist,
The dusk will have its way.

TRAVELING BACK TO SCHOOL

Dry grass running 70 miles an hour
Along freeway curbing.
Dirty car doors flaunting one another.
Unsightly telephone poles.
Insults on mammoth billboards—
A meaningless jumble of words.
Highway regulations of yellow, red, green
And reflective, dirty white.
Cars signaling unintended turns.
Relentless blinking lights.
Birth-pangs of a headache.
Cheap summer drive-ins at long last closed.
Deserted nightclubs.
Despondent churchyards.
The omnipresent railroad-tracks.

WINTER NIGHT DEJECTION

A myriad of thoughts tumbled down on me
Out of starlit heavens,
Thoughts leaping into form
From vast frosted silences;
Thoughts of the infinitesimal meaning of life,
Of hope delayed and love abated,
Of abstinence from society.
Darkling woods questioned my approach
As I stepped out of reach of the yardlight.
Flooding thoughts of loneliness,
Defeat of the human ego;
Sounds of trees creaking and groaning
Under snow and ice,
And wind rising blisteringly through
Tops of evergreen and poplar.

THINGS I LOVE OUT CAMPING

Music of fire.
Freedom to think.
The smell of burning pitch-pine wood.
Smoke from the campfire in my thoughts about God.
The expectation to explore.
Letting the sun be my wristwatch.
The gentle warmth of tender, early morning light.
Conversation with new-made friends.
A camera in my lap,
Pleasure in a nap.
The lines of the trees.
Splendor of blue sky,
An insect passing by.
The joy of luxurious leisure.
The distant clang of horseshoe stakes.
The art of living in the present,
But also thoughts of the remembered past.
The quietude of heart at ease,
Ashes in the breeze.

SUNSET

Listless clouds were stacked
Upon the hearth of the sun,
Waiting to be consumed.
But it was doubtful
If they could all be used that evening.
The fire was dying
And was to be quickly extinguished
By a dark expanse of pines
In the receding distance.
As soon as the flaming rays were gone
The light of the sparks
Shot into the sky,
Igniting the wet cloud-wood
In scarlet smoke.
And then it was too much
For the feeble fire's smoke,
And even it was gone.
Though one could see
Orange ashes in the sky.

III. HAWAII

BAY ON KAUAI

This is my bay today,
A semisphere of sugared sand;
My bay to watch the boats go out,
And feel the waves come in.

This cottage-lined recluse of surf,
The dancing, shimmering sweep
Of easy waves upon the earth,
Of broken shells upon the beach.

Off bronzed skin the salty ocean
Streaming sudden, strong;
On stiffened knees the granuled breeze
Reiterates the song.

Fearless and carefree here
My heart not bound by sorrow;
This is my bay today
Some other one's, tomorrow.

LUMAHAI BEACH

I escaped into a special freedom this morning—
Freedom from myself.
Freedom to be a portion of the ocean,
To scamper lightly over black lava, as the crabs;
Free to let my spirit dash itself up against
The massive face of rock
With each swelling promise of continuity.
Free to wash out to sea
In swirls of sand,
And to return as the scalloped curls of white
Mounted on the peak of each incoming
Dynamic spectacle of splendor.
I escaped into the mirrors of the reflective pools
Stretched out upon plateaus
Of ancient lava flows.
For I had escaped from myself
Into the freedom of the ocean.

SOLDIER IN HAWAII

Such was ours in cherishing the sun,
We came to stake a plot of beach when day began;
To lay a line of beachtowels down,
Secured with lava rocks around.
Such was ours to run unarmed,
Unburdened on the polished sand,
In the eternal summer land.
Thus was the inward motion—
To be with children of the ocean,
Beachbound in the strength of sunshine's warmest quest,
Stretched full length of the soul to dream and rest;
Till having too much of the sun and sand and sound,
We gathered stakes and moved to higher ground.

WITH SOLITUDE

I found it hidden among rock this morning
At Pupukea's lava bouldered shore,
And with a crab as it jumped between rocks
Near the seaweeded play of the waters.
For that infinite moment it was with the crab
As it poised in hesitation—and then jumped.
For then my mind was not on some unfamiliar scene
Or person. It was affixed, there,
Poised in waiting with that crab.
Stilled, waiting for the very next moment of the present
Where only solitude resides.
I felt it as a light sprinkle of rain
Mingled with Hawaiian sunshine
In crazy patterns on my back.
I heard it in the fanciful oceanic clattering
Of currents propelling mystic harmony from loose rocks,
Reverberating through hollowed crannies in
The channeled stone.
I saw it in the purple symmetry of sea creatures,
And the blue-green languor of the swells;
In orange pineneedles
That dropped morosely to the rocky soil.
And then I sensed that it abode in this spot!
But no, some fishermen came and with their shouts
The breeze carried it away.

THE HAWAIIAN SEA

Blue foaming over stolid stone,
And with each breaking crest, the hollow roar.
Against eternity, black lava's claim
To be the utmost tip of shore.
Wave cresting into wave
Upon one common goal bent,
To ask black stone if it will not relent
Such futile claim. Each wave a question.
But lava is content to be;
And bear the image of the sea.
Water plummeting downward on a
Huge crestbreaker walking in,
Submerged seaweed ever flowing
As undercurrents go out again.
An islet of rock becomes a fountainhead
Each time a rising surge anoints its reach.
Surf dancing upon furious surf
As it afflicts the beach.
For a single hour to be free,
With the jagged beauty of the sea.

WITH THE OCEAN

The ocean performs a miracle
Of freedom on the mind;
For there, thoughts flow freely,
Swelling and ebbing as tides and waves
Work wonders with the sand.
And like the sand, old thoughts are pushed about,
New avenues created.
Wind whips loosely through the mind
Clearing out stale chaff
Accumulated from more impoverished days,
Quickening to deeper perception
And more truthful reality.
In the salty splendor of the ocean
Is cleansed away the weak, pretentious
Frame of mind;
For there, only beauty, truth and wonder
Can remain.

SURETY

The lines the sand forms on the mind
By contours of the sweeping beach,
The arctic poles could well compose
Such mystic reach.
The islands of the soul
That stretch from pole to pole
When isolated whole in curl of a wave.
This finite land defines
Infinite designs;
The reaches of a peaceful mind.
Freedom to float free upon the
Prismal, crystalled sea.

CAPTURED DAWN

Gray rose in majesty alone
Up from the surging of the sea,
High hills did not disdain to own
This continuity to me.

Backwaters lay in rock-ringed pools,
Crabs wandered on lonely sand,
A bamboo fishing pole stood frightened,
I was dwelling in a deathless land.

Sun looked in envy
On one precipitous peak and it was over,
The fragile first hours
Of a day in gray clothed honor.

BAY AT WAIMEA

The ocean's salty tongue lapping—lapping
Clear and cold on firm packed sand,
Clear beyond the diamond's glint,
And cold;
A green blue ribbon of transparent glass
Curled lightly by an invisible hand
Of that force greater than the ocean's.
A broken sandcastle—a discarded dream,
And the ocean's pledge to conquer both,
Gently, lapping—lapping.

WAIMEA BAY

Saltspray drifting up against rock cliffs,
There to end its short-lived flight
From thundering waters.
Just off shore at anchor lies a sunken ship of rock,
The noise of seething swells rushing headon
Against stone in mighty claps,
And between the cliff and ocean,
A lonely trampled strand,
Stretching out to the rise on the brink of beach
Where waves meet destiny's demands,
Crushed into silence of bubbling sand.
And here and there on the ocean's side of the rise,
Just beyond reach of the fingers of sweeping foam,
A broken set of tracks is left to abide the time
Until the further moving wave
Obliterates the steps of leisure.
Other than that, there is but one half-formed sand castle
And a blackened, curled arm of driftwood,
Save for a few withered, unknown fruit from the sea,
And the husk of a discarded coconut.

WAIMEA BAY

High surf, and with it churning white,
The whiplashed foam released to break
In chunks and sail a frightened sea.
Returning ere its journey is begun.
Shooting spray, to mingle with the
Clouds; to find a home when it cannot
Abide the sea.
Waves trailing whitewashed banners as
They crest, casting up their inner
Violence of contempt against all
Obstacles of stone.
Foam rushing headlong up, in fashioning
The sand; thus to repent in swifter motion,
Back to the seething ocean.
Saltspray joining with the warming sun to ask
A traveler if his searching life was not begun but
To meditate this moment at the ocean's edge,
Everything else forgotten or found dead.

WAIMEA

I was in and out with the ocean today
In its game of sliding life.
A moment on the peak of a heightened swell
And then its breaking past me with
The backspray catching me full-faced.
The next instant in the depths of the abyss,
Black rocks clattering on the sandy bottom.
The game was to stay with the wave's pursuit
Clear upland where it smoothed the sand,
Then quickly turning with it,
Racing back to sea to float suspended in an
Intermediary world; aesthetic and free
In the engulfing coolness.

LAST DAY AT WAIMEA

This was a fine day for rugged waves,
Surging in anticipation of their winter domination.
Majestic breakers poised to cascade in breaking spray
Over golden gilded rock,
The spray diffused into desperation
Upon the watchful, bouldered cliffs.
This was a fine day for release from the ties of burdened life.
My soul wandered on the peak of the giant shorebreak
And fled down the rising channels of the surface waters,
Chasing itself ahead of the feathered tongues of
Watered beauty on the sand.
This was my last day at Waimea, so I drank of the wonder
At the conception of a future dream.

THOUGHTS OF HAWAII

As breeze in palms in late Hawaiian sun,
So are thoughts in my mind
When I recall the windward ocean
With its whitecapped tales of salt and solitude
Along an endless stretch of pearled, seashelled sand,
And particles of lava of the land.
Or captive magic of eternal tropic night,
When crescent-mooned, the dancing surf
Refracts the silver-slivered light.
The eastward summit of each surfer's dream,
Which approaching mounts with courage
Ere its inner truth is seen.
The preponderant symmetry of swelling wondrous waves.
This will be the memory it brings,
When thoughts of far-away are given wings!

IMPRESSIONS OF THE MIND

(gathered at the ocean)

As rain falls sternly on the beach
Thoughts within fall silently
To where I cannot reach.

As waves roll inward to the sand,
Mind rolls outward from the land.

Wind rises torturously like hope
From the bottom of the soul.

IV. LIFE AND BEYOND

TRANQUILLITY

I was not given the spirit of fear
And hatred of the simple things,
For I was privileged to be there
To trust an insect's wings!

To find a peace and pleasure
In a weathered pine,
Or in an apple grown round a twig,
The leafless woodbine's autumn vine,
The antics of a pig.

I was given the spirit of hope and love
Of the natural quiet place,
The sunbeam's pursuant, gentle charms,
Wild orchid's tiny, vibrant face.

The gray-clad lava rock,
That's seen its share of storm;
The wings of yellow butterfly
That's fragilely reborn.

TIES OF THE CITY

Life of the city was strong in my nostrils. Boys were playing tennis in the street. In the distance, power-mowers chewed at the coming dusk. Taxis scuttled to and fro like rabbits in the brush. It's strange that should occur to me—I hardly knew what rabbits were. There was no time nor need for such things here. There was no need for anything; all was supplied by the city. Emptiness gnawed my bones. I stepped into backyard sunshine. Somehow it felt strange to me and sent a chill to my brain as it warmed me. Something in its background was foreign to the city. I must find it!

The driving was touch and go. Maybe I should have waited until after rush hour. But I couldn't. Finally I was out; way out. Stopping by a fast flowing stream, I discovered a deserted footpath. Many must have walked it before. I tried it. Walking down below the first cataract, I felt the sun bouncing among the droplets as they fell, making the water vibrate where it stretched in pools below. I took a new breath. Mist from the cascade filled my lungs and the life of the city grew dim in my nose!

THE MEANING OF A MOTHER

Mother is the hope to see her children satisfied;
Strength to supply them fortified;
The joy of family fellowship;
The life by which they entered it.
Mother is the life-breath of a child;
The future of a coming world, and mild;
The wisdom in a full-grown son;
The comfort to a daughter, young.
And this Mom's life will not consist of fears,
But must consist of love, and sometimes, tears,
But these are only lent, to cherish
And achieve a betterment for whom they flowed.
Mother's like the rainbow viewed in Noah's time,
In priceless color tone.
Mother is the living symbol of a home.

FROM CHILDHOOD

My parents made me what I am,
An outdoor lad with a little bit of sun.
A boy seen barefoot in a summer rain,
Or fishing, with a bamboo cane;
In the swimming hole with shade,
Or selling homemade lemonade;
A race up meadow hills in fall,
Not being in the house at all,
A summer day.
Trailing deer or hunting ducks
With father, and it was enough.
Childhood's past, these days are done,
And now I am a man
With a little bit of sun.

DEATH'S SORROW

Often pain is scattered as the frost at night,
The morning finds it melted by the joy of light.

Though doubt is present in the drizzling rain,
Yet hope revives when flowers grow again.

When sorrow forms a sky of universal gray,
Peace is born to escort it away.

And weariness is heavy as the snow,
But patience waits to wake new life below.

EVEN A VAPOR

What is your life?
The brief warmth of sunshine on a cloudy day
The ripples from a stone thrown into a placid pool
The glimmer of a lightning-bug
The embers of a fire at night
The joynote of a bird in flight

A cry, for an instant heard above the storm
Loose shingles in a heavy wind
The last flicker of a candlewick, spent
The drifting snow preceding spring
The voice of a violin

A momentary smile in the crowd
A word spoken on the ocean
A grassblade in the sod
The floating seed of milkweed pod

A comet in a universe of space
An elderly insect
An hour's grace
One heartbeat in a race.

BLACK HILLS

Invitation to the Day

The early morning sun makes its first appeal to the
    summit of hills.
It pleads upon the stubborn granite-rocks flung
    among the pineneedles.
As always, it is repulsed, for granite has its own cold life,
Still, though it may be; dormant with a hope.
Sunlight turns its rays unto the fallen, weathered wood
    in masquerade of moss.
The lifeless forms hesitate to make reply unto the sun
And then remain unspoken like the stone.
The opened pinecones on the ground are not to be awakened.
Bullpines talk among themselves and answer to the sun,
    but in tones inaudible.
Soon the sun peers into sheltered valleys, and
    human sounds in camps
Below break up the quiet morning scene.

SHADOW AT SUNRISE

Mount Rainier hunched treetop high in the misty blue distance;
A gray camel in the eastern sky.
The blue was yielding to pink,
Except the swath of sky which the shadow of the mountain
Still held in a mighty effort.
It was a moment to love when early sun
First met crisp silence in the frosted spruce;
A moment when boughs took new day's breath.
Last evening's air had left a dimension of heavy frost;
On everything a different pattern.
Sturdy roughened logs were encased with bark of
Feathered frosty tails;
And spearheaded into a timbered railing,
A million javelins of white crystal glistened in the light.
Frost on an outside tabletop was a jeweled toothpick forest.
Round brown grass stems had become pipecleaners.
The ground was impregnated with a new-formed diamond field,
Pebbles and small stones slightly recessed below earth level.
When I scuffed my boot upon such ground infinite jewels
Avalanched as from an eruption,
And tingling frost reverberated through
Mossed greenness covering entombed elms.

AFTER SUMMER DOWNPOUR

Waiting, throughout the cloudburst,
There was that patch of open sky.
At times the rain came in gushing sheets,
Driven with wind, but was mostly heavy and fast
And came straight as it fell.
The blue sky waited.
The torrents began the gradual cycle of lessening,
Until quite suddenly,
The water had ceased altogether.
Light, resplendent from the rain,
Broke upon everything,
Accenting the purple anger-spent clouds
That were avenged and vanishing.
White infant clouds leaped to replace them
In the changing network of the heavens.
On the street the brave light gently began to clear away
Pools of rain alongside of a girl with braids and a broom;
A youthful streetsweeper of puddles.

REFLECTION

Often we become too tied up in ourselves to think.
When this happens
We lose our greatest potential for living.
We restrain ourselves to life of an animal,
Letting the blessing of being human pass us by.
When we cease to think
We lose our appreciation of beauty.
And when we lose this, we lose ourselves,
And any real friends we could have had.
And we lose one of the qualities
That makes life worth living.
Thought stimulates the mind to purpose and action.
Thought quiets the will to patience and peace.
Thought is the soul of a man!

DESTINY

My life is but a blade of grass
Reluctant of the day
When sun will cease
And winter's blast
Will carry it away.

My heart is but a spider's web
Strung to this fragile frame,
Still it must bear the flow and ebb
Of life's delusive game.

My mind is but the speck that's caught
Within this web of pain,
Yet it gives birth and seeds of thought
Have vestiges of fame.